Sitting at the Feet of Jesus

Finding Rest in a Restless World

Johannes Facius

New Wine Press

New Wine Ministries
PO Box 17
Chichester
West Sussex
United Kingdom
PO20 6YB

Published under license to New Wine Ministries by Sovereign World Ltd.

ISBN 1-903725-59-3

Cover design by CCD, www.ccdgroup.co.uk
Typeset by CRB Associates, Potterhanworth, Lincolnshire
Printed in the United Kingdom

Contents

Foreword

In August 1992 ninety pastors, elders, ministry leaders and intercessors gathered together for three weeks in Canberra desiring to spend time looking to Jesus. As the leaders of the Intercessors for Australia we had invited some significant speakers, one for each week, to help focus us on Jesus. However, none of the selected speakers was able to come, except for Johannes who said he would love to be with us, but only as a delegate as he had never done anything like this before; coming simply to spend time looking to Jesus.

The leadership team met together in prayer before the first meeting anticipating we would receive a guiding word from the Lord for the gathering. However, Jesus remained silent. This continued to happen each day over the three weeks! He was delighted that we had come aside just wanting to be with Him! However, He made it clear that He would only reveal what was on His heart as we gathered to worship Him each day. This was something none of us had experienced before, spending time together without a speaker, and without a program, but simply looking to Jesus! As we worshiped Jesus each day both His word and His Spirit's gifts began to flow amongst us spontaneously as He poured out His Bridegroom love on us. Slowly, lovingly Jesus began to speak about the condition of His body, revealing our independent ways, and exposing our insecurities as we learnt to wait upon Him in stillness and rest.

During a time of worship in the second week Johannes audibly heard the Lord speak to him; "My people do not live in the fullness of what I have done." Johannes spontaneously shared how Jesus wants us to live in all the fullness of what He has already done, and that the fullness of the baptism of the Holy Spirit is intended to make us one body, not just for the impartation of spiritual gifts. At the conclusion of our time together it was evident that the Lord was doing a deep work in our lives drawing us closer to Himself.

Upon returning home to Germany, Johannes confessed that he would never be the same again after spending this time sitting at Jesus' feet! Only by looking to Jesus and waiting to behold Him face to face do we discover true discernment to see situations through His heart and understand His burdens for the Church and the world. Our first priority is to wait until we hear Jesus speak. Only then, under the Holy Spirit's anointing, would we be free to share God's word with others. Johannes was reminded of Jesus' words, *"It is the Spirit who gives life; the flesh profits nothing. The words that I speak to you are spirit, and they are life"* (John 6:63).

One word from the Lord to our hearts can be life-changing, and learning to wait in His presence with expectation until He speaks becomes a sheer joy! And should He not say a word we are content to learn what it means to rest in Him. Under the gentle hand of the Holy Spirit we discover that our "quiet time" will be radically changed. The words He speaks to us are transformed into words of life as we meditate on Him in the Word. Our prayers will have an anointing we have not known before, finding ourselves echoing the very prayers on Jesus' heart. This will not happen overnight, but as we offer Jesus quality time, sitting at His feet becomes a way of life, communing Spirit to spirit. Being content just to be with Jesus is truly liberating!

Since 1992 we have regularly met with others to sit at Jesus' feet in a number of nations. Each gathering has been uniquely different as Jesus has sensitively ministered both to individuals and to the group. People continually confess their busyness and their desire for a deeper love relationship with Him. They long to discover more of the wonder of His person. Repeatedly they ask, "Now that I have tasted a new-found intimacy with Jesus how do I grow in this relationship with Him?" These stirrings of our hearts are a great joy to Jesus, who is ever ready to draw us closer to Himself.

Johannes' book focuses on some foundational teaching to help us discover the essentials in learning to sit at Jesus' feet. He highlights many of the problems that we continually encounter and exposes a lot of our misconceptions. Johannes brings clarity to us with the cutting edge of Jesus' words and his own perceptive insights. Unless we grasp these practical guidelines from God's Word there will always be a battle going on in our minds as we try to hear Jesus speak to us. It is from the place of worship, adoration and meditation that our minds are quickened to gather His word as food, nourishing our spirits and teaching us to hear His voice and understand His ways. This is where real change takes place!

Noel and Barbara Bell
Sydney, Australia

Why are you entranced by the spirit of the world? Why do you concern yourself with things too profound for you? A lukewarm love will never know the heart's passion for the Bridegroom.

Where are the hungry hearts waiting for the kiss of His Word? Stir up love! Stir up love, O Bride, your lamp lacks oil, the oil of His strong Bridegroom love. Without this you will never last the night!

When the storm descends upon your house will it stand? Have you built on the sands of sincere labour for your Lord, or on the secure rock of hearing His voice, and knowing His love?

Do you know the warmth of His embrace, His gentle words of love upon your heart? Is it not time to come aside to delight in His presence, to quietly rest in His arms, and hear Him whisper, "How fair and lovely you are, My beloved"?

O Bride, come now, set your work aside. Come into the secret place and sit at His feet to wait patiently, listening for His words of life. With growing expectation come and worship your Lord. He will surely meet you there!

Then the flickering flame of love in your heart will be gently kindled to glow brighter and brighter into a fire of passionate love for the only One to whom you are betrothed. Come!

Listening to God

Chapter 1

One Thing Needed

The story in Luke 10:38–42 about Jesus' visit to the home of Mary, Martha and Lazarus in Bethany is most familiar to all believers. This home is considered by many as Jesus' only earthly home where He often visited and rested whenever He passed through Bethany on His many travels into or out of Jerusalem.

When on this particular day recorded in Luke 10 as Jesus visited, Mary rushed to sit at the feet of Jesus, while Martha, her sister, continued with attending to the many practical things that needed to be done in the house. We often think that the problem here is a matter of resting versus working. Mary was resting at the feet of Jesus whereas Martha was busy running around in the house to prepare things. I don't think it speaks about a choice between resting and working, or between devotion and serving. We all know that we need both times of resting and times of working. I am pretty sure that Jesus did not mind that Martha was preparing food and making things comfortable for Him at His visit. I do believe we do Martha wrong when she is portrayed as an altogether negative figure. It is much more a choice between a condition of peace of mind or an anxious and stressful mind. The Lord Jesus, I think, is pointing out the great importance of right priorities rather than just condemning Martha and commending Mary.

We can learn much from considering the difference between these two personalities. Martha seems to have been a strong person since the passage in Luke 10 tells us that it was Martha who welcomed Jesus into *"her house"*. Truly the house belonged to all three of them but Martha seems to be in charge of the household. This indicates that she was the dominant person used to taking the lead and getting the needed things done. You could say that in Martha we find a strong, independent personality ruling her own life as well as the people in her household.

Mary, who rushed to sit at Jesus' feet to listen to the Master's words, appears to have been of a more gentle, weak and dependent nature. Probably also more undecided and insecure, needing the advice and the direction of others. The behavior of these two women caused the Lord to make these discernments:

Martha, He said, was distracted with much serving. She was distracted from seeking intimacy with the Lord and giving first priority to fellowship with Him. Her activities produced in her inner being worries, anxieties and even frustration and anger as she blamed her sister for not assisting her in doing the needed things in the house. It was not the things that had to be done that Jesus was displeased with. It was the attitude of Martha and the anxiety of her heart which derived from the fact that unlike Mary she did not give priority to the presence of her Master. Her anxious and troubled heart was a direct consequence of failing to first come and sit at the feet of Jesus before she went on with her work.

When Jesus entered the house, the first thing Mary gave the Lord was her undivided attention. It would be wrong to assume from this that Mary, in the course of daily life, was totally uninterested in participating in the work in the house and doing her part. We are not talking about a choice between doing practical work of serving the Lord and devoting our-selves to having intimate communion with Him. We are talking about having the right order of priorities in our walk with God. As Mary sat at the feet of Jesus listening to His word a deep sense of peace, security and assurance flowed into her heart. It gave her the spiritual strength and direction needed for the day. Jesus said that Mary had chosen the good part, which would not be taken away from her. He also said that what Mary did in coming to sit at His feet was the one thing needed. According to this there is actually only one thing that is really needed: to come and sit at the feet of Jesus. There are many things important in the life of the believer, many things that should be done, but there is according to the Lord Jesus only one thing needed: to sit at His feet and listen to His word as the first and foremost thing that must be practiced. We should all learn the lesson of hearing from God first before hearing from anyone else!

We should also heed the words of Jesus about this matter being a choice we have to make. Jesus said about Mary that she had chosen the good part. So often we think that being in the will of the Lord will automatically provide us with that inner peace and strength that we need for every day. It does not work that way. We have a choice to make whether or not we want to cease from our activities and for a while come to sit at Jesus' feet. Only as we learn to make time and space for communion with the Lord by an act of our will shall we be delivered from the troubles and the anxiety that would otherwise seek to dominate our innermost being.

His word brings inner peace

The Scriptures speak about the importance of knowing how to fill ourselves with the Word of God. In Paul's letter to the Colossians we read these words:

> *"And let the peace of God rule in your hearts, to which also you were called in one body; and be thankful. Let the word of Christ dwell in you richly in all wisdom, teaching and admonishing one another in psalms and hymns and spiritual songs, singing with grace in your hearts to the Lord."*

(Colossians 3:15–16)

To me there is a direct connection between letting the word of Christ dwell richly in you and having the peace of God ruling in your heart. When the word of Jesus enters your heart it brings with it the peace of God and the consequence of that is that your inner being comes under the control and protection of the Spirit of God. The ruling of God's peace will also provide you with the ability to make the right choices and find the right directions for your way forward.

The word of Christ entering your spirit and dwelling in your mind and heart is an immensely powerful thing. Hebrews 4:12 puts it this way:

> *"For the word of God is living and powerful, and sharper than any two-edged sword, piercing even to the division of soul and spirit, and of joints and marrow, and is a discerner of the thoughts and intents of the heart."*

There is such a need to be able to filter our own desires and thoughts and to come to an understanding of what is of God through the Spirit and what is of our own soulish nature. How would we ever be able to know what comes from God and what comes from ourselves or any other source unless we let the word of God dwell in us? There are so many Christians today who are unable to discern what happens, and they end up in confusion and even enter into many different sorts of spiritual deceptions. The present time in which we live is full of all kinds of spiritual experiences and manifestations that are doubtful when seen from a biblical point of view. How are we ever going to avoid becoming victims of the winds of false doctrines and practices blowing through the modern church today unless we know how to come and sit at the feet of Jesus and listen carefully to His word, letting His living and powerful word cut through all the thoughts and intents of the human heart?

There is such a wonderful promise connected to coming and sitting at the feet of Jesus and turning all our attention to His marvelous person and word. Listen to these words from the book of Isaiah:

"You will keep him in perfect peace,
Whose mind is stayed on You."

(Isaiah 26:3)

The connection between rest and work

There is never a choice between rest and work, but there is a choice between how to accomplish our work for God with a peaceful heart having come to rest in God, or serving the Lord with a troubled heart filled with anxieties and frustrations.

How is the work of God being done? The disciples at the time of Jesus were taken up with this question. This is what they wanted to know from Jesus.

> *"Then they said to Him: 'What shall we do, that we may work the works of God?' Jesus answered and said to them, 'This is the work of God, that you believe in Him whom He sent.'"*
> (John 6:28–29)

It might appear to be a rather strange answer by Jesus to a very straight question from His disciples. The disciples wanted, of course, practical instruction about how they could do the works of God. Instead Jesus points out that the way God's work is carried out is through having an intimate relationship with the Son of God. It is through such an ongoing close communion with the Lord that the direction, the motivation and the empowerment to serve the Lord and do His works flows. Corrie ten Boom, also called God's Globetrotter, once said: "If you want to work for God, don't hesitate to establish a committee. But if you should desire to work with God, don't hesitate to form a prayer group." This really tells the difference between the way of Mary and that of Martha. Mary sat at the feet of Jesus listening to His words, and she was motivated, empowered and directed to serve the Lord in close fellowship with Him. Martha was serving, basically, out of her own initiative and according to her own plan. God's work can only be done God's way and under the specific guidance of

His Holy Spirit. Knowing this truth could save us from a lot of our own self-appointed effort which would lead to much trouble and anxiety and ultimately could have us ending up burnt out.

His works or ours

When Jesus taught His disciples about the true Vine in John's gospel chapter 15 He underlined the truth that our interaction with the Lord is based on a relationship with Him and not on any external set of rules and regulations. He repeatedly stressed that we need to abide in Him continually and if we do not we can do nothing of spiritual value. When our Lord encourages us to abide in Him He also indicates that it is possible not to abide in Him. This means that we can either be connected to the Lord or disconnected. The responsibility for this lies with us. It is an almost daily choice we need to make to decide to abide in the Lord or not. That continued or discontinued intimate communion with the Lord determines whether we are going to be fruitful in our work and ministry for God. To me, abiding in Jesus is just another way of saying that we need to come and sit at the feet of Jesus if we want to walk in God's ways and do the works of God.

Our "doing" would have to flow out of an intimate fellowship with Him if it were to accomplish anything meaningful in the Kingdom of God. In calling His disciples He spoke these words:

> *"You did not choose Me, but I chose you and appointed you that you should go and bear fruit, and that your fruit should remain, that whatever you ask the Father in My name He may give you."*   (John 15:16)

It should be almost self-explanatory that we never chose Jesus, but that indeed He was the one who chose us. Nevertheless, it so often appears that we act as if we had chosen the Lord as we seek to get the Lord's approval and blessings upon our own ideas and plans. Sometimes it looks as though we really believe that God was created for our sake and that He is only there to serve our every need and bless our various activities. Nothing could be further from the truth. We are the ones created for His pleasure and glory and our deepest desire should be to serve His plans and purposes on earth.

Jesus said that He chose us and appointed us to go and bear fruit. Here is something important to consider. For us to have a fruitful life and ministry we need to make sure that we are doing what He has appointed for us. Actually there is no other way in which we can bear fruit than doing what the Lord has called us to do. As my friend Lance Lambert used to say: God will not bless or support non-commanded work! If we are into non-commanded things we would have to do them in our own power. We cannot rely on God's help or His power for anything for which we have not been appointed. I remembered from my own life and ministry how in my younger days I desired the ministry of an evangelist, or if I could not have that I would like to have the gift of healing. I saw how these ministries would attract the big crowds. I did try to become an evangelist but I never succeeded. It became a hard burden upon me to try and I hardly ever saw anyone coming to the Lord and being saved through my work as an evangelist. The reason is clear: I had not been appointed by the Lord for this work and could therefore claim no anointing and power for that ministry. Lots of frustrations, disappointments and quite some discouragement came from my well-meaning attempt to serve the Lord in a field that was not His appointed work for me. I was like Martha serving the Lord without having sat down first at His feet and received His words and instructions. Being in non-commanded work has become the most common reason for thousands of Christians, the Lord's servants, ending up burnt out.

Also notice that Jesus spoke of bearing fruit, not of achieving results. Modern Christianity has been impacted so much by worldly thinking that we almost behave like businessmen. We want to see results of everything we do, as though that is the only thing that matters. We are counting numbers of people attending our meetings, numbers of funds entering the offering boxes, size of meeting halls etc. One would think that we are in the business of selling something! Jesus speaks about bearing fruit. Fruit is different from results. Results are the outcome of activity, but fruit is the outcome of a relationship. Results can be produced quickly and they can disappear just as quickly. Fruit takes a long time to produce and it only comes forth through the life flow of an intimate relationship. The Lord wants fruit and fruit that remains! He is not interested in any temporary success. Remember that it is only the fruit that we can bring with us into eternity. Our spiritual gifts and their performance in this world cannot enter eternity, only that spiritual character that has been built into our innermost being by the transforming power of the Holy Spirit.

His burdens or ours

It is the burdens that we take upon ourselves that weigh us down, not the burdens that the Lord puts upon our lives. When people experience burn-out and indicate that their depressive condition is due to their hard work in the Lord's service, I do not believe a word of what they are saying. Does anyone really believe that it is the Lord's intention to kill His servants by overloading them with work and responsibilities?

Listen to this word of the Lord Jesus:

> *"Come to Me, all you who labor and are heavy laden, and I will give you rest. Take My yoke upon you and learn from Me, for I am gentle and lowly in heart, and you will find rest for your souls. For My yoke is easy and My burden is light."*
>
> (Matthew 11:28–30)

Although these verses are often used to preach the gospel to sinners, there is no doubt that these words were primarily spoken by Jesus to His disciples. It is clear that if anyone labors and becomes heavy laden it is not because he or she is serving

God the way they should. It is because they are staggering under a wrong yoke and struggling to carry burdens that have not been put upon them by God. God's yoke is easy and His burden is light so therefore they could never break anyone to pieces or send them into a position of total burn-out.

We are not talking about rest being a condition with no work, no effort and no sweat. Jesus was a man who worked a lot. He talks about a twelve-hour working day. He walked extensively, attended to multitudes of needy people and often He spent the night in prayer to His heavenly Father. But you never see Jesus troubled, anxious or discouraged, with the sole exception of His final battle in the garden of Gethsemane. The Lord never suffered any burn-out experience. The reason for this is clear: He only did what His Father asked Him to do. His lifestyle is clearly laid out through this declaration:

> *"Most assuredly, I say to you, the Son can do nothing of Himself, but what He sees the Father do; for whatever He does, the Son also does in like manner."* (John 5:19)

Jesus would only take upon Himself the burdens that His Father wanted Him to bear and He would only walk under the yoke which His Father had put upon Him. Because of that, He had His Father's support and the sustaining upholding power of the Holy Spirit right through to the end. Also we can walk without being broken down and heavily laden when we learn to take our burdens from the Lord and walk in the yoke of His will for us through this life. His yoke is easy and His burden is light and will never cause us any burn-out experience.

To His wondering disciples Jesus once said:

> *"My food is to do the will of Him who sent Me, and to finish His work."* (John 4:34)

Eating food is not supposed to wear us out and leave us weak and exhausted. On the contrary it is meant to stimulate us and give us renewed strength and power to do our work with gladness. What stimulated the Lord Jesus and kept Him strong and vibrant through His many works was the fact that He was walking in the ways appointed for Him by God, the Father. If we would take the time to come and sit at the feet of Jesus to fellowship with Him and receive His words, we also would know what He has appointed for us, and be able to walk in the strength of the Spirit through the day and through our whole life.

Chapter 2

The Battle for the Mind

The problem of distractions

What kept Martha from coming to sit at Jesus' feet and listening to Him was that she *"was distracted with much serving"* (Luke 10:40). When we come to sit at the feet of Jesus we will find that it is not an easy thing. There are many things that would try to distract us from hearing His voice. There is a battle going on in the mind to try to get control over our thoughts and to direct our full attention towards the Lord. Like Martha we too suffer from many distractions. For many Christians it has become quite a problem to concentrate. We live in a time where our brains are being bombarded with heaps of stuff almost twenty-four hours a day. The intensity of the modern information society requires our constant attention and we feel more and more caught up in the business of this life. It is a problem that will increase as we enter into the last days of this age. Jesus warned us to beware of this danger:

> *"But take heed to yourselves, lest your hearts be weighed down with carousing, drunkenness, and cares of this life, and that Day come on you unexpectedly. For it will come as a snare on all those who dwell on the face of the whole earth. Watch therefore, and pray always that you may be*

21

> *counted worthy to escape all these things that will come to*
> *pass, and to stand before the Son of man."*
>
> (Luke 21:34–36)

It is interesting to me that Jesus compares drunkenness and the cares of this life (in other versions called "the business of this life"). The reason for this must be that being caught up in the business of this life will have the same effect on us as being drunk. A drunken person has his senses reduced. He does not know where he is or where he is going and he does not know what is going on around him. Being sucked into the business of this life can have the exact same effect on a person. I think it is true to say that the vast majority of God's people do not have a problem with drunkenness. Sad to say, the same is not the case when we speak of being entangled in the business of this life. Modern Christians generally have great difficulty in knowing how to wind down and come to a place of silence where they can be available to hear from God. Unless we find a way to deal with distractions we will never be able to come and sit at the Lord's feet and receive His words, because people with a preoccupied mind won't get anything out of a time with the Lord.

Distractions are, however, not just a natural problem. They are something that the enemy of our souls is trying to impose upon us whenever he can. I believe the devil is working overtime to try to distract us from ever hearing from God. As someone who has preached and taught the Word of God for many years in churches all over the world I have been able to observe the reactions among the people. Often I have seen people who would constantly look around in the church, or look repeatedly at their watches or even yawn openly while we were worshiping or while I was speaking. It was clear to me that they might be physically present in the church, but in their minds they were miles away. They were being distracted from enjoying the presence of God and from hearing the Word. For quite a while I excused this phenomenon as natural. Could be that people were tired after a long day or bored stiff with my presentation. Then one day I had another look at this scripture:

> *"Therefore humble yourselves under the mighty hand of God, that He may exalt you in due time, casting all your care upon Him, for He cares for you. Be sober, be vigilant; because your adversary the devil walks about like a roaring lion, seeking whom he may devour. Resist him, steadfast in the faith . . ."*
>
> (1 Peter 5:6–9)

It has become clear to me that not all distractions are just due to natural causes. There is a massive attack by the devil upon God's people to try to overwhelm them with anxieties, accusations and various forms of distractions in order to pre-occupy them in their mind so that they cannot hear from God. The devil is walking about, and mind you, he is not walking down the streets of our big cities. He is walking around in the church among the people of God. His aim is to devour the saints.

To me the best way to explain what "to devour" means in this context is that the devil tries to preoccupy the minds and hearts of the believers. This is a deliberate strategy from the powers of darkness. If the enemy can succeed in fully "block-ing" out our minds then it does not matter even if we should try to come and sit at the feet of Jesus. We would not be available to commune with the Lord and to hear what He wants to speak to us.

The way he does this work of blocking our minds and ears from hearing God is through what the Word here calls "cares". As we saw earlier cares are the same as being sucked into the business of this life. The devil is busy putting so many concerns upon us from our busy life that we often end up worrying ourselves to pieces. That is why the apostle Peter here advises us to "cast our cares upon Him [the Lord]". That seems to be the way we can resist the devil; being firm in the faith. "Casting" means "to take action against the worries which are filling our thoughts". One big problem we have as believers is that we have not yet fully understood that worrying is not a natural human thing which we can excuse. Anxiety in the Word of God is a sin because it is an expression of unbelief. When we worry about things in life we are in fact showing distrust in our God and dishonoring Him and the work of salvation He has done for us. Not until we learn to treat anxiety as a sin can we really cast it out of mind and heart and get rid of it.

For many years I have had a diary in my study that was made by secular businessmen. For each day there is a kind of proverb to read. None of it is Christian. For one particular day it reads:

> "Some people instead of drowning their worries are teaching them to swim!"

How true this is. So often we let our worries stay in our mind and let them grow until they fully possess us. We should follow Peter's advice to cast them upon the Lord. We shall see a little later in more detail how we can do that. It is important that we understand that our distractions to a certain degree are being imposed upon us by the devil. The enemy is not against religious activities as long as we never get to the point where we enter the presence of God and begin to hear His voice. In a scripture from the book of Daniel that speaks prophetically about the anti-Christian period before the coming of the Lord it says:

> *"He [the anti-Christ] shall speak pompous words against*
> *the Most High,*
> *And shall wear out the saints of the Most High."*
> (Daniel 7:25, NKJ Lit. translation)

So the devil is busy these last days trying to overwhelm and wear out the saints of the Most High in order to make us burned out and thus useless for serving the purposes of God and His Kingdom.

Thoughts can be dangerous

Thoughts can be dangerous. Actually everything begins with a thought. There has never been an ideology or theology or even an invention that did not start with a thought in somebody's head. The same goes for sin. Sin starts in the thought life and if nothing is done about it at that stage it will eventually result in a sinful act. Judas Iscariot, the disciple who betrayed his Master Jesus, is a good example of what we are talking about here.

The Scripture says that during the last supper Jesus shared with His disciples before He went to the cross, Satan *"put it into the heart of Judas ... to betray Him* [Jesus]*"* (John 13:2). At a later stage during the actual sharing of the wine and the bread when Jesus handed a piece of bread to Judas, it says that *"Satan entered him"* (verse 27). Already, for some length of time, Judas had given the devil access to his heart by repeatedly stealing money from the disciple's money box. Judas had been trusted to look after the finances and he became a thief out of his greed for money. Satan cleverly used this sin to tempt Judas with even more money as he agreed to betray Jesus for thirty pieces of silver.

Although we all know that the case of Judas' betrayal was in a way predestined, it does not take away from the principle behind the actions. What began as a thought in his mind grew and grew until the devil got him totally in his power and drew him to betray Jesus and afterwards to take his own life in deep despair over what he had done. Suppose Judas had dealt with the thought at the initial stage? That might have enabled him to seek repentance and deliverance from evil. This should be a warning to all of us that we deal with even the smallest sinful thought entering our mind before it takes root in our heart and starts growing into sinful acts.

Thoughts can dominate our whole personality and if we identify with them in our heart they will provide us with our very identity as persons. Listen to this word from the book of Proverbs:

"For as he thinks in his heart, so is he."   (Proverbs 23:7)

It is a fact that the way we think about ourselves will somehow provide us with our very identity. A lot of Christians are suffering under the impact of wrong thoughts – wrong thoughts about themselves and wrong thoughts about God. We need to be aware of having wrong thoughts about ourselves both when the issue is about feeling inferior or about feeling proud. Inferiority complexes as well as proud thinking can in the end ruin our lives. How much better it is to identify with God's thoughts about us. In God alone do we get the right and true identity. Listen to this wonderful word from God to His chosen people:

> *"For I know the thoughts that I think toward you, says the* LORD, *thoughts of peace and not of evil, to give you a future and a hope."*   (Jeremiah 29:11)

It all depends on how we learn to deal with our thought life, rejecting that which is not of God and coming to the feet of Jesus to receive His word. We will have more to say about this when we explain the importance of learning to empty ourselves and to meditate upon the living Word of God.

Martin Luther when speaking about thoughts once said:

> "You cannot prevent a bird from flying over your head, but you can prevent it from landing upon your head and start building a nest."

He is touching on a spiritual reality here, namely that our minds are laid open to be accessed by multitudes of thoughts flying around in the air. This "open mind" is part of God's creational purpose with us. If it were not so we would never have a choice between good or evil and we could not be tempted by sin. Even this fact is explained to us on the very first pages of the Bible. The serpent had access to Eve's mind:

"Now the serpent was more cunning than any beast of the field which the Lord *God had made. And he said to the woman, 'Has God indeed said, "You shall not eat of every tree of the garden"?' And the woman said to the serpent, 'We may eat the fruit of the trees of the garden; but of the fruit of the tree which is in the midst of the garden, God has said, "You shall not eat it, nor shall you touch it, lest you die." ' "*

(Genesis 3:1–3)

We know what happened. Eve was being impacted by a false thought that if she ate the fruit of the forbidden tree, she would be just like God. As she did not reject that thought from the very outset she was tricked into taking another look at the fruit of the tree. She saw that the fruit was good for food and that it was pleasant to the eyes, and that the tree was desirable to make one wise. The thought overpowered her and together with her husband Adam she took of its fruit and ate. The failure of this first couple on earth to properly discern and filter away the false and evil thought injected into their minds caused the greatest tragedy in human history from which all living people have suffered throughout the entire history of the human race.

Chapter 3

Making Yourself Available

Dealing with distractions

As we have seen, we cannot get any benefit from sitting at the feet of Jesus unless we deal with all that distracts us. A preoccupied mind full of concerns and worries about thousands of daily matters will prevent us from getting in touch with the Lord and hearing His words. We need therefore to know how we can clear out our mind and empty it from all distractions taking our thoughts captive to the obedience of Christ. The Word of God offers us some help in doing that. There are some tools we can use to bring our mind and our thoughts under control. One such tool is to practice confession. A wise man of God once said that the way to get things out of your heart and mind is through your mouth. He also said that the way things enter into your inner being is through your ears.

A key word to know the power of confessions is found in Paul's letter to the Philippians:

"Rejoice in the Lord always. Again I will say, rejoice! Let your gentleness be known to all men. The Lord is at hand. Be anxious for nothing, but in everything by prayer and supplication, with thanksgiving, let your requests be made known to God; and the peace of God, which surpasses all

understanding, will guard your hearts and minds through Christ Jesus."

(Philippians 4:4–7)

I always used to think when reading these words that it is easy for Paul to say that we should rejoice always. He even repeats it to make it firm. The Word of God, though, is true and would never make a statement like this if it was not possible to put it into practice. A life of constant rejoicing, however, requires that we can come to the place where we are anxious for nothing. Joy and anxiety do not go together. Therefore we must be able to find a way where we can get rid of our worries if we are ever going to "rejoice always". And sure enough, there is such a way provided for us: *"in everything by prayer and supplication, with thanksgiving, let your requests be made known to God."*

The way to kill our worries is to practice what Paul here instructs: to let everything be made known to God. Here we often have a problem. Can we really tell God everything? The word here encourages us to verbalize our worries, our requests and even our wishes to God. Sometimes we feel that we could not do a thing like that. We need to only express "holy" things to God and never our deepest frustrations and feelings of discouragement or strong desires. I think this kind of "religious" attitude is the very reason why we never get our inner man cleaned up from all the wrong thoughts and selfish desires. Remember that the only way we can get things out of our hearts and minds is through our mouth.

I have always admired the prophet Jonah. He seems to have had a very frank and open relationship with God, and he was not afraid of expressing even his disapproval with the way God acted in the case of Nineveh. Remember how God commanded Jonah to go to Nineveh and bring His message because the inhabitants of the city had angered the Lord through their many sins. Jonah, however, did not obey God because he did not want to get unclean by going to these sinful pagans. To mingle with these kinds of people was not according to the

Jewish tradition. Jonah therefore rejected God's call and went on holiday instead, buying a ticket to go by ship to Tarshish from Joppa. This journey would take him in the opposite direction from Nineveh, and what he did not realize was that it would also take him away from the presence of the Lord (Jonah 1:1–3). It is, however, not possible to get away from the Lord's calling. The Lord sent a great wind, so that the ship was about to be broken up. Jonah ended up being thrown overboard and the Lord most kindly let a big fish pick him up and return him to where he should have gone to begin with: to the shores near Nineveh. Jonah then fulfilled his commission and preached God's Word to the inhabitants of Nineveh: *"Yet forty days, and Nineveh shall be overthrown!"* (Jonah 3:4). We all know the rest of this remarkable story. The people of Nineveh repented of their sins, and God decided to forgive them and to spare the city from destruction. That greatly upset Jonah. After all the trouble he had gone through to be made willing to deliver God's message of judgment he must have felt that God had exposed him to be a false prophet. This is how he reacted:

"But it displeased Jonah exceedingly, and he became angry. So he prayed to the LORD, and said: 'Ah, LORD, was not this what I said when I was still in my country? Therefore I fled previously to Tarshish; for I know that You are a gracious and merciful God, slow to anger and abundant in lovingkindness, One who relents from doing harm.'" (Jonah 4:1–2)

One would have thought that Jonah's anger would have upset God, and that He would have sent fire down from heaven to consume His rebellious prophet. But the Lord just kindly corrected Jonah and taught him a great lesson. I believe that we should, like Jonah, dare to make known to God how we feel even when we disagree with Him or are even angry at Him. Unless we verbalize what is in our heart we will never be released from thoughts and emotions which would block our minds and stop us from being able to be free to listen to the voice of the Holy Spirit.

The apostle James is encouraging the saints to regularly come together and practice confession:

> *"Confess your trespasses to one another, and pray for one another, that you may be healed."*   (James 5:16)

Healing here does not only refer to physical sickness but also to a sound and a healthy mind. The word "healed" also means "to be restored to normal". We therefore need to use confession and prayer to make sure we are released from whatever tries to preoccupy our innermost being. Prayer is like the breath of the believer. We inhale the Word of God and the Spirit and we exhale all the wrong thoughts and emotions that would block our mind and heart. This is the way our physical breath is working: we inhale fresh oxygen and we exhale the poisoned stuff that has assembled in our lungs. We need this kind of spiritual recycling and Philippians 4:6–7 describes this process which I call practicing "mental hygiene". The wonderful result of practicing this is not that we get everything we ask from God, but that the *"peace of God, which surpasses all understanding, will guard* [our] *hearts and minds through Christ Jesus"*. There is nothing that can be compared with the inner peace of God which comes when we openly confess our anxieties and any other burden that weighs us down. It is a peace that fills our hearts and minds even in matters where we have still not got any answers to our questions. That is why it is called a peace which surpasses our understanding.

Commanding your soul

Have you ever thought about taking charge of your mind and soul? As born-again believers we are supposed to rule both our soul and our body through our spirit, our spirit being indwelled by the Holy Spirit. All too often we give in to being dominated by the desires of the soul and the body. Paul is instructing us to bring *"every thought into captivity to the obedience of Christ"* (2 Corinthians 10:5). The important thing is to know the answer to the question "How do we do that?" Also when Peter speaks about resisting our adversary steadfast in the faith, we need to know how we can do that. I suggest to you that this can be done through learning to take control over our soul and to use the power of the proclamation of the Word of God.

King David had a habit of speaking to his own soul as recorded in many places in the book of Psalms. In Psalm 42:5, 11 and in Psalm 43:5 he says this:

> *"Why are you cast down, O my soul?*
> *And why are you disquieted within me?*
> *Hope in God, for I shall yet praise Him*
> *For the help of His countenance."*

David will not allow his soul to sink down into self-pity or resignation. He is commanding his soul to trust in the Lord.

In Psalm 103:1 he says:

> *"Bless the Lord, O my soul;*
> *And all that is within me, bless His holy name!"*

Through this whole psalm David is reminding his soul of all the blessings God has poured out upon his life and he is directing his soul to bless the Lord for all His goodness and mercy.

In Psalm 116:7 he says:

> *"Return to your rest, O my soul,*
> *For the Lord has dealt bountifully with you."*

Here David speaks about all the tribulations and troubles he encountered being oppressed by his enemies almost even unto death. But by God's help he was delivered and he now instructs his soul to return to its resting place in God.

In the same way he takes charge over himself in Psalm 131:2 and orders his soul to be calm and quiet before the Lord:

> *"Surely I have calmed and quieted my soul,*
> *Like a weaned child with his mother;*
> *Like a weaned child is my soul within me."*

We should learn not to allow ourselves to become victims of any thought or emotion that is not from God, but take them captive and put them under the authority of Christ as we command them to be subject to His lordship.

Proclaiming the Word

Proclaiming the Word of God is the weapon we have been given to fight against the powers of darkness. When the devil attacks us, and he is doing that all around the clock because he is the *"accuser of our brethren"*, accusing God's people day and night (Revelation 12:10), we need to use our weapons of warfare against him. Paul instructs us to lift up the shield of faith whereby we can quench all the fiery darts of the wicked one and to operate the sword of the Spirit, which is the Word of God (Ephesians 6:16–17). We do that by proclaiming the powerful living Word of God.

The Word of God teaches us that we have the authority to silence the enemy:

> *"Out of the mouth of babes and nursing infants*
> *You have ordained strength,*
> *Because of Your enemies,*
> *That You may silence the enemy and the avenger."*

(Psalm 8:2)

Far too often we allow the enemy to harass us and bombard us with his thoughts and his accusations. It is as if we do not think we can do anything about it. But we can. As truly as we have become the children of God through being born again by His Holy Spirit we have received the ability and the authority to silence the enemy.

I remember how, in my younger days, I used to suffer from thoughts of fear and accusation. On one particular occasion I had been summoned to appear before the local tax authorities after I had submitted my tax papers. This had never happened before so I feared that I had been caught in making some false statements about my income. This fear grew within me more and more and it took away my peace. I was not aware of having done anything wrong, and I did not know why I allowed myself to be harassed by these accusing thoughts over a period of several weeks. One morning as I was reading my Bible I came across this word from Psalm 8, that God had established strength out of the mouth of His children to silence the enemy. It dawned upon me that I had to open my mouth and use the authority that had been given to me against these fearful thoughts. I remember that I went into our bedroom and closed the door. At the top of my voice I made a strong proclamation against the enemy and ordered him to shut up and leave me alone. Immediately I was delivered and could breathe freely again. A few minutes later the bell rang at our entrance door. As I opened the door our friendly neighbor was standing there asking me if everything was OK with us. Apparently everybody in the whole apartment building had heard my proclamation! Sure enough, when I appeared before the people in the tax office there was not the slightest problem. They only, very kindly, wanted to inform me that I had forgotten to deduct some of my travel expenses which would reduce the amount of income tax I was due to pay.

Chapter 4

Directing Your Mind

When we have emptied our mind from all distractions and preoccupations, we are ready to come and sit at the feet of Jesus and listen to His word. We are ready to do the only thing needed, to devote our undivided attention to the Lord and direct our mind to concentrate on Him. The practical way of doing this is to engage ourselves in what we call Bible meditation. Our aim is to focus our mind on Him. It is important not only to get rid of all the negative stuff that occupies our mind but also to learn how to fill our mind with all the good things of the Lord.

Bible meditation is very different from any other kind of meditation because it never leaves us with a mind that is empty and void. Jesus teaches us that we must never just cast out evil spirits from a person. We must make sure that such a person is being filled with the Spirit. This is what the Lord has to say about this vital matter:

> *"When an unclean spirit goes out of a man, he goes through dry places, seeking rest; and finding none, he says, 'I will return to my house from which I came.' And when he comes, he finds it swept and put in order. Then he goes and takes with him seven other spirits more wicked than himself, and they enter and dwell there; and the last state of that man is worse than the first."* (Luke 11:24–26)

In trying to focus our mind we should never meditate using our own thought processes or let our mind wander into thin air. We should not even think about Jesus out of our own imagination. We meditate on Him through His Word.

Before we proceed further let us make clear that all meditation is powerful, even the meditation that happens on the wrong side of the fence. We can open ourselves up to powerful demonic religious spirits if we practice our meditation in any other way than in the Lord and through His Word. That meditation can have a strong effect on people's lives is beyond any doubt. I came to know a story about a non-believing businessman in the city of Copenhagen, where I was born. He was the manager of a business employing many people. He lived a very stressful life and ended up in a burn-out situation. A friend of his suggested to him that he consult with the local TM center and have a talk with the guru. The guru gave him this unusual advice that he should arrive every morning in his office before anyone else came and bring a little fresh flower with him. He then should lean back into his arm chair, put his feet up on his desk, take the little flower and sit starring at it for twenty minutes while he repeated again and again: "What a wonderful little flower you are!" After having done so for a couple of weeks the manager learned to control his mind and his stress level was reduced considerably. Through this experience, however, he came under the influence and impact of the Indian guru and his occult teachings.

We have something that is much better and safer than things and mantras from Hinduism. We have a living and risen Savior and the pure uncorrupted living Word of God.

It is important that we learn how to concentrate and focus our mind upon Jesus. In Matthew 6:22–23 we read these words of Jesus:

> *"The lamp of the body is the eye. If therefore your eye is good (footnote: clear, or healthy), your whole body will be full of light. But if your eye is bad* [footnote: evil, or unhealthy], *your whole body will be full of darkness."*

The King James original version reads: *" ... if therefore thine eye be single ... "*

I believe that the Lord speaks here about the importance of having a clear focus, a clear vision and to make sure that our eyesight is not blurred or out of focus. The use of the word "single" in this connection gives me the understanding that we need to be single-minded people. You know the word of the apostle James where he speaks about the need to be cleansed from being double-minded:

> *"Draw near to God and He will draw near to you. Cleanse your hands, you sinners; and purify your hearts, you double-minded."* (James 4:8)

And James continues with this matter of being double-minded by reminding us that a double-minded person should not suppose that he will receive anything from the Lord (James 1:7–8).

Our success in entering into the presence of God and being able to touch Him and hear His word as we come and sit at His feet depends on learning how to discipline our mind and direct it with full concentration on to Him. Bible meditation will help us to achieve this. We need to learn how to meditate upon the Lord through His Word and not just read the Word in a hurry or throw a quick glance at Him. It is not enough to think about the Lord. We need to meditate on Him. The difference between thinking and meditating is a matter of time. We shall consider this subject in more detail later in this book. It is enough to add here that meditating can be compared to operating the focusing ring on a pair of binoculars. It takes a bit of time to get a sharp and a clear picture. The two lenses need to blend together and form a single clear image for your eyes to enjoy. If the focusing facility does not work properly you will be left with an unclear double image.

Denis Clark and Campbell McAlpine, these two great men of God, from whom I learned so much, used to illustrate the practice of Bible meditation with a cow lying in a field and chewing grass. The cow has four stomachs. When the cow picks the grass from the field it starts chewing. After a while the grass goes down into the first stomach. From there it comes up again for another chewing and flows down to the second stomach in a more refined condition. This process continues four times until the grass is so refined that it can be fully digested, and the result is wonderful life-giving milk for us all to enjoy.

When we meditate we pick a relatively small portion of the Word of God and we start reading it slowly and carefully while we pray for the Holy Spirit to speak personally to us. The idea here is to repeat the reading of this portion over and over again until something is being highlighted in our mind by the Spirit and we sense the Lord is speaking to us. In this way we are disciplining our mind to concentrate upon what we are reading, operating our spiritual focusing ring until we get a clear image, a clear enlightenment of our mind to understand and receive what God is speaking to us. This process takes time and we will quickly discover that if we do not take the time that is needed we won't get anything out of coming and sitting at the feet of Jesus. How much time is needed is of course a very individual matter, as it is easier for some people to concentrate more quickly than others.

Chapter 5

Consider Jesus

To practice Bible meditation we are in need of two things:

1. an object for our meditation,
2. making time available for it.

The object of Bible meditation is not a beautiful little flower, nor is it actually the Bible. It is the person of the Lord Jesus.

The passage from Philippians 4:4–9 is such a key to understanding Bible meditation that I want to quote it here in its full length:

> "Rejoice in the Lord always. Again I will say, rejoice! Let your gentleness be known to all men. The Lord is at hand. Be anxious for nothing, but in everything by prayer and supplication, with thanksgiving, let your requests be made known to God; and the peace of God, which surpasses all understanding, will guard your hearts and minds through Christ Jesus. Finally, brethren, whatever things are true, whatever things are noble, whatever things are just, whatever things are pure, whatever things are lovely, whatever things are of good report, if there is any virtue and if there is anything praiseworthy – meditate on these things. The things which you learned and received and

41

heard and saw in me, these do, and the God of peace will be with you."

The first part of this passage (verses 4–7) as we have seen deals with emptying our mind from all anxiety, and in doing so we will obtain true peace of mind. The peace of God, which goes far beyond our understanding, will guard our minds and hearts in Christ. In this way we shall enjoy a true and lasting condition of inner peace, the peace of God.

In the second part (verses 8–9), when we learn to fill our mind with all these good, pure, just and lovely things mentioned here, we shall experience *"the God of peace"* being with us, and that will work as an active force to lead and guide and empower us on our way forward.

By saying *"meditate on these things"* I don't think Paul is speaking about good things in general, such as nature, art and music. I don't think anyone can claim the company of the God of peace by just meditating on any positive subject. I don't think Paul is referring to the modern day doctrine of "positive thinking" either. He is not referring to things in the realm of the soul, although all of such good things undoubtedly can have a good influence. Here we are dealing with spiritual things, because Paul is referring to *"the things which you learned and received and heard and saw in me"*. What could everyone learn and see in the apostle Paul? They could see the character and nature of Christ, the Lord. It is Jesus who encompasses every good, pure, just, lovely and noble thing. We are to meditate upon the glorious character of the loveliest, most wonderful and perfect person in the whole universe: the Lord Jesus Christ!

Let us consider some scriptures to that end:

> *"Therefore we also, since we are surrounded by so great a cloud of witnesses, let us lay aside every weight, and the sin which so easily ensnares us, and let us run with endurance the race that is set before us, looking unto Jesus, the author and finisher of our faith, who for the joy that was set before Him endured the*

cross, despising the shame, and has sat down at the right hand of the throne of God. For consider Him who endured such hostility from sinners against Himself, lest you become weary and discouraged in your souls." (Hebrews 12:1–3)

Here, once again, we find the two sides of the practice of sitting at the feet of Jesus. The negative part of laying aside everything that burdens us, and every sin. When we have dealt with that we exercise the positive part, to look to Jesus and to consider Him.

We are to consider Jesus not only in His past sufferings and His death but also to see Him as the One who now sits at the right-hand side of His Father. A major aspect of meditating on Christ is to consider His perfect finished work: His incarnation, His life on earth, His crucifixion, His ascension and His glorification, being given all power and authority both in heaven and on earth.

The word "consider" is more than just "to think". The word "consider" is of the same meaning as the word "meditate". Another word we could use is "to contemplate" or "to dwell on". To think of Him, often means just to get a quick glimpse of Him, whereas the other words involve more time. The wonderful outcome of considering Jesus in His finished work of redemption for us is that we will not *"become weary and discouraged in* [our] *souls"*. Practicing Bible meditation is the only real way of avoiding stress, anxiety and discouragement, and to be kept in a condition of ongoing peace of mind.

Listen to this wonderful word of the Lord:

"You will keep him in perfect peace,
Whose mind is stayed on You." (Isaiah 26:3)

Notice the word "stayed". This word only works for those who have learned to fix their minds on the Lord in a continual way.

It is the exact same meaning in the next word we will consider from 2 Corinthians 3:18 – 4:1:

"But we all, with unveiled face, beholding as in a mirror the glory of the Lord, are being transformed into the same image from glory to glory, just as by the Spirit of the Lord. Therefore, since we have this ministry, as we have received mercy, we do not lose heart."

What is "this ministry" that can keep us from "losing heart"? It is to behold the glory of the Lord with an unveiled face. An unveiled face is nothing else other than walking in the light, having all one's sins forgiven and being covered by the blood of Jesus, so that there is nothing clouding our communion with the Lord. And the glory of God is nothing else, or should I say no one else other than the glorious Son of God, our Lord and Savior. For He (Christ) is the brightness of God's glory and the express image of God's person, and upholds all things by the word of His power (Hebrews 1:3). We see God's glory when we see Christ, and if we do not see Christ in one another or in the church fellowship we don't see God's glory at all. To make the glory of God a feeling or a particular experience or event is nothing but charismatic imagination.

As we consider Jesus and do it long enough, for the word here is to "behold" which is also more than having a quick glance, what we are beholding will impact us and change us into the same image. Therefore who ever practices "this ministry" will never lose heart.

The mirror it speaks about here can only mean the Word of God. For where else is the person and character of Christ portrayed but in the Scriptures? We are not to sit and imagine who Jesus is in our own selves. We are to come to know Him as the One who reveals Himself and His true nature and character in the Holy Scriptures.

James, the apostle, confirms this in the first chapter of his epistle:

"For if anyone is a hearer of the word and not a doer, he is like a man observing his natural face in a mirror; for he observes himself, goes away, and immediately forgets what kind of man

he was. But he who looks into the perfect law of liberty and
continues in it, and is not a forgetful hearer but a doer of the
work, this one will be blessed in what he does."

(James 1:23–25)

What can the perfect law of liberty mean other than the pure
Word of God? That is the mirror that we all have to look into.
But only he who "continues" to do so will experience how the
Word will impact him and change him into the likeness of
the Son of God. The blessing it speaks of here will only be ours
if we learn to continue to meditate on the powerful Word of
God.

Consider Jesus in the Word of God

In Bible meditation we do not give you a painting of Jesus or
an orthodox icon to look at, and we do not ask you to close
your eyes and try to imagine Jesus. We ask you to open the
Bible and in reading the Word of God to find the many aspects
of the wonderful person of Jesus and of His wonderful
redemptive work. It is the Word of God that portrays who
the Lord Jesus really is.

The best way, of course, is to listen to what the Lord says
about Himself in the Scriptures:

> *"Then He said to them, 'O foolish ones, and slow of heart to*
> *believe in all that the prophets have spoken! Ought not the*
> *Christ to have suffered these things and to enter into His*
> *glory?' And beginning at Moses and all the Prophets, He*
> *expounded to them in all the Scriptures the things concerning*
> *Himself."* (Luke 24:25–27)

From this we learn that Christ is the overall subject of the
Scriptures. The entire Word of God gives extensive testimony
to the character and work of our wonderful Savior and Lord.
We can see Him everywhere in the Book and we can hear Him
speak to us through the Word.

What we need is to have the same experience the two disciples of Jesus had on the road to Emmaus:

> *"And they said to one another, 'Did not our heart burn within us while He talked with us on the road, and while He opened the Scriptures to us?'"*   (Luke 24:32)

For us to come to see Jesus and to hear Him through reading the Word we also need the Holy Spirit to open up the Scriptures to us. This is what Jesus did for all of His disciples before He departed from them after His resurrection and ascended into glory:

> *"Then He said to them, 'These are the words which I spoke to you while I was still with you, that all the things must be fulfilled which were written in the Law of Moses and the Prophets and the Psalms concerning Me.' And He opened their understanding, that they might comprehend the Scriptures."*
>   (Luke 24:44–45)

The whole aim of Bible meditation is to sit at the feet of Jesus and meditate on His Word for as long as it takes for our understanding to be opened by the Holy Spirit. We need more than an open Bible; we need an opened mind. That is why we talk of both the Word and the Spirit.

Jesus once said this when He answered the Sadducees who claimed that there is no resurrection:

> *"You are mistaken, not knowing the Scriptures nor the power of God."*   (Matthew 22:29)

You see, it is important to know both the written Word of God and the power of the Holy Spirit who alone can open our minds to understand it. This is what Jesus underlined when He said this to His disciples:

"You search the Scriptures, for in them you think you have eternal life; and these are they which testify of Me. But you are not willing to come to Me that you may have life."

(John 5:39–40)

This is why we do not meditate on the Bible but on Jesus, who is our risen Lord and Savior, and who is the central subject of all Scriptures.

The work of the Spirit

It is the work of the Holy Spirit to give us the Word, to open up the Word, and to reveal Christ to us in the Word:

"I still have many things to say to you, but you cannot bear them now. However, when He, the Spirit of truth, has come, He will guide you into all truth; for He will not speak on His own authority, but whatever He hears He will speak; and He will tell you things to come. He will glorify Me, for He will take of what is Mine and declare it to you. All things that the Father has are Mine. Therefore I said that He will take of Mine and declare it to you." (John 16:12–15)

It is important for us to understand the role of the Spirit in relation to the Word of God. The Bible is in itself just a book and we must learn not to make it into something magic, just as if the very letters of the Bible are containing divine life. Such an understanding of the Bible is not only false, but it can lead to much error and to dead legalism and fundamentalism. We must beware of what someone called "Bible-idolatry". The book is not God, and if we treat it as such we can do much damage to ourselves and to other people. How we need to depend on the Holy Spirit and allow Him to lead us into all truth. Through Bible-meditation we give time to wait upon the help of the Holy Spirit as we read the book and to allow Him to open up the Word for us and make it alive to us.

Paul very clearly differentiates between what he calls the letter and the Spirit:

> *" . . . but our sufficiency is from God, who also made us sufficient as ministers of the new covenant, not of the letter but of the Spirit; for the letter kills, but the Spirit gives life."*
>
> (2 Corinthians 3:5–6)

Never try to handle the Word with your own understanding and to use it out of your own desire or will. It won't work for you. There is a lot of so-called proclamation of the Word of God that comes out of the soulish realm. Proclaiming this and that word from the Bible without having received it from the Holy Spirit, without that word having been given to us by the Spirit of God. The charismatic world is full of all kinds of misuse and even abuse of scriptures and the sad thing about it is that it never works. When will we ever learn to come to sit at the feet of Jesus and wait upon Him to speak His living Word into our spirit? The letter kills, but the Spirit gives life. But some would say: "Didn't Jesus proclaim the Scriptures against the devil when He was being tested in the wilderness?" Yes, He did but, mind you, before He entered the wilderness He returned from the Jordan filled with the Spirit and was led by the Spirit into the wilderness (Luke 4:1). If Jesus our Lord needed to be filled and led by the Holy Spirit in order to use the Word of God as a powerful weapon, how much more do we need to be under the complete control and guidance of the Spirit, when we issue any proclamation of God's Word!

There is a lot of talk about doing things by faith and sometimes one gets the impression that we automatically have the faith do everything we want to. Let us never forget from where faith comes:

> *"So then faith comes by hearing, and hearing by the word of God."*   (Romans 10:17)

So much misunderstanding about the exercise of faith comes from not reading this word correctly. Faith does not come by the Word of God; it comes from hearing, and the hearing comes out of meditating upon the Word. It is very possible to read the Word and not to hear anything and very often the reason for that is that we do not give time enough in the Word but are grabbing the Word by our own understanding and trying to make it work. The only faith that is alive and powerful and will accomplish what it sets out to do is the faith that comes out of hearing the voice of the Holy Spirit. If we don't hear anything we are left with a word that is dead without any divine power. I can never emphasize strongly enough what Jesus said, that we are mistaken because we do not know the Scriptures nor the power of God, which is the Holy Spirit.

Chapter 6

Waiting on the Lord

A successful outcome of sitting at the feet of Jesus and listening to His Word depends on the amount of time we are ready to spend in Bible-meditation.

The Scriptures deliver a clear message that only those who wait on the Lord will be able to claim the blessings of entering the presence of the Lord.

> *"Blessed is the man*
> *Who walks not in the counsel of the ungodly,*
> *Nor stands in the path of sinners,*
> *Nor sits in the seat of the scornful;*
> *But his delight is in the law of the* LORD,
> *And In HIs law he meditates day and night.*
> *He shall be like a tree*
> *Planted by the rivers of water,*
> *That brings forth its fruit in its season,*
> *Whose leaf also shall not wither;*
> *And whatever he does shall prosper."* (Psalm 1:1–3)

Here we find the great blessings of practicing Bible-meditation. Notice though that the condition is to meditate day and night in God's Word. It is the time factor that is important here. A superficial or casual reading of the Word of God cannot produce the spiritual fruitfulness it speaks about in this psalm. The one who meditates this way will grow his roots deep down into the plenteous supply of the river, and he will be able to produce fruit in the season and his leaf will never wither, and most of all: he will prosper in whatever he does. A similar portion of God's Word we find in Jeremiah 17:7–8:

> *"Blessed is the man who trusts in the LORD,*
> *And whose hope is the LORD.*
> *For he shall be like a tree planted by the waters,*
> *Which spreads out its roots by the river,*
> *And will not fear when heat comes;*
> *But its leaf will be green,*
> *And will not be anxious in the year of drought,*
> *Nor will cease from yielding fruit."*

I think we are dealing with a very important truth here. Are we root-Christians or rain-Christians? By this I mean that as believers we can either grow deep roots into Christ and make sure that we will have a constant supply of the water of life, or we can try to live from the more sporadic spiritual showers of blessings we can obtain from time to time.

Let me illustrate this. Many years ago I lived in Copenhagen and was part of the leadership of a church. One of the elders was a medical doctor. He was also very gifted in many other areas. During one summer we suffered from a long drought which dried up the land in many ways. One Sunday my friend invited me and my wife to dine with them after the service in the church. Because of the drought he had to water his garden every day to prevent the plants and the flowers from dying. I went out in the garden with him before we sat down to eat dinner and followed him as he walked around to water the flowers from a bucket. I suddenly discovered that he jumped over one small little bush with wonderful yellow flowers. I immediately turned to him and said: "What has this little bush done to not deserve a splash of water?" He then explained to me that this particular bush he had brought home with him from the Negev desert in Israel. "This special bush", he said, "has deep roots. In fact its roots under the surface are much longer than the plant above the soil. If I begin to water the bush it will take this as a sign that it does not have to continue growing its roots further down until it hits water underneath." "That is why", he said, "I don't water it from above even during a severe drought!"

I immediately learned a spiritual truth from this event. We have two kinds of believers when it comes to seeking blessings from God. We have those who have taken the effort of growing spiritual roots down into the riches of God's Word. They have become people who are no longer dependent on whatever external blessing or spiritual experience they can get from anywhere such blessings might be offered. They are people who no longer are in need of being constantly prayed for or counseled every week in the church. They know how to draw from an inner supply of the Holy Spirit through an intimate personal relationship with the Lord and through maintaining a continual habit of sitting at the feet of Jesus.

The other category of believers consists of people who are on the run always trying to find blessings here and there. We have Christian people who are roaming around on the planet to places where there seems to be some kind of revival going on through which they might get some help. They often end up discouraged when they discover that you cannot import God's power and the fullness of His Spirit that way. You will have to dig down and grow roots into Christ through meditating on His Word and then you will have a constant supply of spiritual strength following you wherever you go.

Think about such wonderful blessings for those who meditate on the Law of the Lord night and day. They will be like a tree whose leaf shall not wither but remain green, and who shall bear a fruit which remains. They shall not fear when the heat is turned on them. They shall not be anxious in times of spiritual dryness.

The Bible likens those who wait on the Lord to eagles:

"Even the youths shall faint and be weary,
And the young men shall utterly fall,
But those who wait on the LORD
Shall renew their strength;
They shall mount up with wings like eagles,
They shall run and not be weary,
They shall walk and not faint."   (Isaiah 40:30–31)

The eagle is an incredible bird. Although it has the biggest wingspan it only very seldom needs to use it. The eagle is also a very clever bird. It lives high up on the mountains, higher up than any other kind of bird. Somehow the eagle knows about the special character of the mountain wind. It knows how the wind in the mountains has a strong drift upwards. When the eagle wants to fly up high it sits on the cliff and waits until it can sense the wind blowing up. It then throws itself out and spreads its enormous wings out to their full width, and lets itself be carried upwards without using any movements of its powerful wing muscles. It only uses its wings as a rudder to steer itself on the way up. A fully grown eagle can soar from very low to a height well above three kilometers without using any energy of its own. It makes clever use of the energy of the wind.

This is what the prophet Isaiah is speaking about. There is a supernatural energy available for us. This is the power of the Holy Spirit. If we learn to wait on the Lord we will open up ourselves to the power of God. It is all a question of what kind of energy we are on: the natural one or the supernatural one? That is what the prophet is seeking to explain when he speaks about the young ones fainting, becoming weary and stumbling and falling. Our own power will not bring us far on our spiritual journey, even those of us who are in the prime time of power and energy. We cannot make it through human effort. There are many young servants of the Lord who end up in spiritual and physical burn-out. How different it is with those who wait on the Lord. They shall renew their strength and mount up with wings of eagles. They shall run and not be weary; they shall walk and not faint. If I have learned anything in my long walk with God it is that it is crucial to make sure that we walk and run in the energy of the Holy Spirit. We can only get access to His power when we learn to wait patiently on the Lord. I am sure this was what Jesus meant when He gave His disciples this instruction:

> *"Behold, I send the Promise of My Father upon you; but tarry in the city of Jerusalem until you are endued with power from on high."* (Luke 24:49)

The Lord did not want His disciples to walk and run and work in their own natural strength and energy, because they would not go far. They needed to know how to walk, run and work in the power of the Holy Spirit. We need that too, today.

Also the Lord Jesus is likening the work of the Spirit to the wind:

> *"That which is born of the flesh is flesh, and that which is born of the Spirit is spirit. Do not marvel that I said to you, 'You must be born again.' The wind blows where it wishes, and you hear the sound of it, but cannot tell where it comes from and where it goes. So is everyone who is born of the Spirit."* (John 3:6–8)

It is clear to me that this describes two different kinds of energy: the flesh, and the Spirit. We are told by Jesus that the flesh never can be anything but flesh. In John 6:63 Jesus declares that the flesh profits nothing. What comes out of our own ideas, visions and dreams and all our own natural effort is equal to nothing. It is nothing but a waste of time; but that which is born of the Spirit is spirit, and the Spirit according to Jesus' word gives life. How are we then to make sure that we are driven by the energy of the Holy Spirit? How can we experience being carried forward by the supernatural power of God?

We are back in the picture of the eagles and the wind. The wind, Jesus says, is sovereign: it blows where it wishes and you don't know where it comes from or to where it goes. We cannot take charge over the Holy Spirit. I know that there is a teaching and practice in the charismatic world of ordering the Holy Spirit around. It is pure wishful thinking and very close to being an offense against the Spirit of God. It is the Spirit who will order us around. We cannot even figure out the way of the Spirit. How then can we enter into the energy of God's power? The secret lies in this phrase: *"... and you hear the sound of it"*. When we learn to wait on the Lord, to meditate long enough on His Word there will come a moment when we sense the move of the Spirit. We will hear that still small voice and make ourselves ready to follow the direction of the Holy Spirit. To come and sit at the feet of Jesus is a practical way of entering into the flow of the Spirit. If only we could learn to take the time to wait upon the Lord.

Chapter 7

Hearing the Voice of God

One of the greatest problems we face as believers is to know how to hear the voice of God. Lots of Christians are battling with this problem every day. And yet being able to hear God's voice is crucial if we are going to make it through the tough times lying ahead of us.

Hearing to overcome circumstances

When we think about the trials and tribulations the Bible tells us will come upon us in the very last days of this age, it becomes important to know how we are able to come through and even overcome such difficult circumstances. To me the only real security we have lies in the ability to hear God's voice.

When Jesus prophesies over the church in His seven letters to the churches recorded in the book of Revelation, chapters 2 and 3, He says two things to all of the seven churches:

1. *"He who has an ear, let him hear what the Spirit says to the churches."*
2. *"He who overcomes . . . "*

To me these two are interlinked in this way, that in order to overcome the circumstances we need to be able to hear the voice of the Holy Spirit.

When we think about the prophet Elijah who is the type of the end-time prophetic calling of the church, this is the way he was able to overcome the drought that lasted three years and six months:

> *"Then the word of the* L<small>ORD</small> *came to him, saying: 'Get away from here and turn eastward, and hide by the Brook Cherith, which flows into the Jordan. And it will be that you shall drink from the brook, and I have commanded the ravens to feed you there.' So he went and did according to the word of the* L<small>ORD</small>*, for he went and stayed by the Brook Cherith, which flows into the Jordan. The ravens brought him bread and meat in the morning, and bread and meat in the evening; and he drank from the brook. And it happened after a while that the brook dried up, because there had been no rain in the land.*
>
> *Then the word of the* L<small>ORD</small> *came to him, saying: 'Arise, go to Zarephath, which belongs to Sidon, and dwell there. See, I have commanded a widow there to provide for you.' "*
>
> (1 Kings 17:2–9)

There are vital lessons to learn from this story. First we need to acknowledge that whenever God sends times of trouble on the land, we believers will have to share the difficulties with the non-believers. The famine in Israel in the time of Elijah did not only hit the people of Israel, but even Elijah himself. The drought that came on the land even hit the little brook so that it dried up and Elijah had to hear afresh from the Lord for his continued survival. Another thing we need to understand from this story is that there is no way we in the natural can figure out how to come through and overcome in the last days. Elijah could never in his wildest imagination have figured out that his survival would consist of a small brook, a bunch of ravens and a poor widow from Zarephath. Only because he had an ear to hear was he able to overcome the circumstances.

We, likewise, would never be able by our human thinking to prepare for what lies ahead. We simply do not know what is coming in any detail, let alone when it will be coming. Therefore we also will have to depend entirely upon God's supernatural guidance and provision. But how will we be able to understand the way He is leading us unless we can hear the voice of the Holy Spirit? It does not pay to make a lot of human calculations based on our own speculations. In my opinion making a lot of practical preparations for something we don't really know about is a waste of time and money. What we do need is to know how to hear from God. That is the only secure and effective way of preparing on a day-to-day basis for the things that lie ahead.

Elijah knew the still small voice of God in his heart. When later in his life he fled out into the wilderness for fear of Jezebel, the wife of King Ahab, he turned to the Lord in prayer. This is how the Lord answered him:

> *"Then He said, 'Go out, and stand on the mountain before the Lord.' And behold, the Lord passed by, and a great and strong wind tore into the mountains and broke the rocks in pieces before the Lord, but the Lord was not in the wind; and after the wind an earthquake, but the Lord was not in the earthquake; and after the earthquake a fire, but the Lord was not in the fire; and after the fire a still small voice. So it was, when Elijah heard it, that he wrapped his face in his mantle and went out and stood in the entrance of the cave. Suddenly a voice came to him, and said, 'What are you doing here, Elijah?'"* (1 Kings 19:11–13)

When the Lord moves there are often supernatural manifestations that go before Him. That was true then as it is true today. We often make the mistake of trying to find the Lord in the manifestations instead of coming to the place where we can hear His voice. If then we only experience certain manifestations but never get hold of the message God wants to bring to our hearts we have missed the mark. It is a good thing to ask the question when we are presented with spiritual manifestations: What did the Lord say through this? Because if there is no message coming through to our hearts one way or the other we have not met the Lord. The Lord is not in the experience. He comes to us through His voice. What we need to look for and if needed wait for, is that still small voice sounding in our hearts. Then we are ready to stand up and go out into wherever the Lord is directing us.

Jesus gives us an important lecture about what matters when we encounter the trials and tribulations lying ahead:

> *"Therefore whoever hears these sayings of Mine, and does them, I will liken him to a wise man who built his house on the rock: and the rain descended, the floods came, and the winds blew and beat on that house; and it did not fall, for it was founded on the rock. But everyone who hears these sayings of Mine, and does not do them, will be like a foolish man who built his house on the sand: and the rain descended, the floods came, and the winds blew and beat on that house; and it fell. And great was its fall."* (Matthew 7:24–27)

Once again there is no way that we can avoid the rain, the floods and the strong winds beating on our house. This will all come upon us in due time. The only way to go through these tribulations is to have an ear to hear what the Lord is saying and then to obey His word. In Jewish thinking hearing is not just hearing. It includes doing what you hear. Once you have obeyed the Word of the Lord you have really heard Him. There is no other foundation that will hold through the coming storms other than the one that is built on the teachings of Jesus, on the Word of the Lord. As I see it, it is about time we make sure that we, both as individuals and as the church, are solidly founded on the rock of the Word of God. When the great troubles come upon the earth it might be too late to lay the right foundation for our lives and ministries. I am greatly disturbed when I hear believers claim that we do not need to be so biblical these days. Some new teachings and practices being promoted in modern Christianity today are based on sand.

Hearing to overcome the enemy

In the battle against the powers of darkness it is essential that we are able to hear from God. Trying to take on great spiritual powers in our own wisdom and strength could prove fatal. We need to have God's strategy in order to overcome the attacks of the enemy.

The kings of Israel understood this. Therefore they usually inquired of the Lord before they entered into battle. In cases where they didn't, the people of Israel would suffer defeat.

David, more than any other, understood this vital matter of hearing from the Lord. Therefore he was very successful in his war against the Philistines. At one point, recorded in 1 Chronicles 14:9–16, the Philistines attacked Israel twice:

> *"Then the Philistines went and made a raid on the Valley of Rephaim. And David inquired of God, saying: 'Shall I go up against the Philistines? Will you deliver them into my hand?' The Lord said to him: 'Go up, for I will deliver them into your hand.' So they went up to Baal Perazim, and David defeated them there. Then David said: 'God has broken through my enemies by my hand like a breakthrough of water.' Therefore they called the name of that place Baal Perazim. And when they left their gods there, David gave a commandment, and they were burned with fire.*
>
> *Then the Philistines once again made a raid on the valley. Therefore David inquired again of God, and God said to him: 'You shall not go up after them; circle around them, and come upon them in front of the mulberry trees. And it shall be, when you hear a sound of marching in the tops of the mulberry trees, then you shall go out to battle, for God has gone out before you to strike the camp of the Philistines.'*
>
> *So David did as God commanded him, and they drove back the army of the Philistines from Gibeon as far as Gezer."*

This is a remarkable story. Certainly no-one would do warfare this way out of his own thinking and wisdom. God's thoughts and ways are indeed much higher than ours. We cannot figure them out with our own limited understanding. I believe we need to learn some most important lessons from this story in order that we might know how we may also overcome the forces of darkness coming against us today. It is all about being able to hear the voice of God and being willing to wait before God until we get the go-ahead and receive His strategy for the battle. One major point is that God never repeats Himself. He does not need to repeat Himself or the way in which He works. David understood this. Therefore he did not take God's go-ahead from the first battle and apply it to the second. He did not assume that since the Lord had given the Philistines into his hand the first time, He would most certainly do the same the second time. No, David knew he had to inquire of the Lord every time he was faced with the enemy. If he hadn't, the army of Israel would not have been able to drive the Philistines out.

We do not always realize how dependent we are on God and how dependent we are on hearing His voice on a continual basis. So quickly we establish our own pattern and think that we have *carte blanche* to go against the enemy and claim the victory over him at any given time. This idea represents a grave misunderstanding that will lead us into all kinds of misconceptions of spiritual warfare. Many so called "faith teachings" have led to spiritual presumption and a world of unreality where things are being claimed and proclaimed that are never happening, all because we do not inquire of the Lord and wait until we "hear the sound of marching" telling us that the Lord has gone out before us to rout the enemy. As we saw earlier: *"the wind blows where it wishes, and you hear the sound of it, but cannot tell where it comes from and where it goes. So is everyone who is born of the Spirit"* (John 3:8). If we do not hear anything from God we have no way to overcome the enemy's subtle attacks against us. We cannot proclaim anything by faith unless God has given us what to proclaim and when to proclaim. The reason is simply that we have not got any faith to operate on, unless we have received a word from the Lord. This is the way true faith works:

> *"So then faith comes by hearing, and hearing by the word of God."*   (Romans 10:17)

Some believers read that faith comes by the Word of God. But they are lacking an important in between: the hearing! We can pick all the Bible verses we like and try to throw them after the enemy, but if the word was not given to us by the Spirit for any particular situation it won't work. The dynamic, divine faith we need to overcome the enemy comes by hearing the word from the Spirit, not just picking a word from the Scriptures.

But you say to me: did not Jesus battle down Satan in the wilderness by quoting scriptures? Yes He did. The scripture, however, clearly states that when He did so, He was specifically led by the Holy Spirit into the battle against Satan:

> *"Then Jesus, being filled with the Holy Spirit, returned from the Jordan and was led by the Spirit into the wilderness, being tempted for forty days by the devil."*   (Luke 4:1–2)

When we also are being filled with the Spirit and being led by the Spirit into the battle against the powers of darkness, we shall also be able to effectively use the Word of God against the enemy. Without the clear guidance of the Holy Spirit we can never be authorized to speak the word and proclaim defeat over the enemy. How would we know how to do this unless we are hearing the voice of God?

Hearing for fullness of life

How do we get to live in the fullness of the Holy Spirit? There is only one way according to the Word of God. It is not through any particular formula, or through following a special spiritual therapy. It is by hearing the voice of God on

a continual basis. Paul puts in this way, writing to the church
in Galatia:

> *"This only I want to learn from you: Did you receive the Spirit*
> *by the works of the law, or by the hearing of faith? Are you so*
> *foolish? Having begun in the Spirit, are you now being made*
> *perfect by the flesh? Have you suffered so many things in vain*
> *– if indeed it was in vain? Therefore He who supplies the Spirit*
> *to you and works miracles among you, does He do it by the*
> *works of the law, or by the hearing of faith?"*
>
> (Galatians 3:2–5)

Through hearing the voice of God we receive an inflow of the
life and the power of God's Holy Spirit. There is no other way
to live in the fullness of the life-giving Spirit of God.

Hearing for divine power

We have already considered this subject. Faith comes by
hearing, and hearing comes from the Word of God. God's
faith does not reside naturally within us. We do not have
divine faith in our human nature. We have human faith like
all people have to a certain extent, but that faith does not
work in the spiritual realm. When we try to operate our own
faith by carnal means it will fail to produce anything of
spiritual or supernatural value. We need to hear from God
and walk in obedience to His directions. Then we shall have
the faith that can move mountains. Paul, the apostle, tells
about an experience of God's healing power, when he was
preaching the gospel in a town called Lystra in Asia Minor:

> *"And in Lystra a certain man without strength in his feet was*
> *sitting, a cripple from his mother's womb, who had never*
> *walked. This man heard Paul speaking. Paul, observing him*
> *intently and seeing that he had faith to be healed, said with a*
> *loud voice, 'Stand up straight on your feet!' And he leaped and*
> *walked."*   (Acts 14:8–10)

As this crippled man heard the voice of God through Paul's preaching, he received the divine faith that led to his miraculous healing.

A similar experience is recorded in the book of Acts chapter 3. This is where Peter and John see a lame man lying down at the gate of the temple called the Beautiful. The apostles ask this man to look at them, and then in the name of Jesus Christ of Nazareth command him to rise up and walk. When Peter takes him by the right hand and lifts him up, he is healed and leaps and walks around in the temple praising God. When the crowd sees this they want to worship Peter and John. This is how the apostles responded to this cheering crowd:

> *"... why look so intently at us, as though by our own power or godliness we had made this man walk?"* (Acts 3:12)

And later in the same chapter:

> *"... the faith which comes through Him* [Jesus] *has given him this perfect soundness in the presence of you all."*
>
> (Acts 3:16)

Notice the phrase: *"the faith which comes through Him"*. It is clear that the Holy Spirit gave to Peter and John the divine faith for this miracle.

Hearing for guidance

According to the Word of God the Lord wants to lead His people and to give them direction by His voice.

This is what the Lord says through the prophet Isaiah:

> *"Your ears shall hear a word behind you, saying,*
> *'This is the way, walk in it,'*
> *Whenever you turn to the right hand*
> *Or whenever you turn to the left."* (Isaiah 30:21)

So if we have ears to hear we should be able to have the guidance we need in our walk with God, whether we speak about our personal guidance or the way the church should be moving.

Philip, the evangelist, had that experience in his walk with the Lord. He was preaching the gospel in Samaria when suddenly he heard the voice of an angel directing him to go to another place:

> *"Now an angel of the Lord spoke to Philip, saying, 'Arise and go toward the south along the road which goes down from Jerusalem to Gaza.'"* (Acts 8:26)

When Philip walked down this road he spotted a man sitting in his chariot, reading the prophet Isaiah.

> *"Then the Spirit said to Philip, 'Go near and overtake this chariot.'"* (Acts 8:29)

The wonderful end of this story was that the Ethiopian man sitting in this chariot was saved and baptized, and it is said that he returned to Ethiopia and was used by God to establish what later became the Coptic Church. What a marvelous example of what it is to be directed and led by the Holy Spirit. Also, Philip experienced a supernatural bonus for his obedience to the voice of the Spirit. He was caught up by the Spirit and was found in Ashdod preaching the gospel (Acts 8:39).

At the start of the apostle Paul's first mission trip, which eventually took him to Europe, it had not been planned by any mission board or committee a long time ahead. It was something that happened when the leaders of the early church were seeking the Lord in prayer and fasting:

> *"Now in the church that was at Antioch there were certain prophets and teachers: Barnabas, Simeon who was called Niger, Lucius of Cyrene, Manaen who had been brought up with Herod the tetrarch, and Saul. As they ministered to the*

Lord and fasted, the Holy Spirit said, 'Now separate to Me Barnabas and Saul for the work to which I have called them.' Then, having fasted and prayed, and laid hands on them, they sent them away.'' (Acts 13:1–3)

This great missionary venture was initiated when the leaders in Antioch heard the voice of the Holy Spirit. Actually they did not have it in mind to make any such journey. At least that is not recorded in Scripture. Their aim was simply just to come together and worship the Lord and to seek His face.

Corrie ten Boom, who was called the Lord's globetrotter, once said: "If you want to work for God, please don't hesitate to form a committee. But if you want to work with God, please hurry to form a prayer group!" The work of the ministry, the work of any mission, is not ours. If it is, it will fail ultimately. It must be the Lord's work if we are going to see it bringing any lasting spiritual fruit. What is not initiated by God will have no chance to overcome the tests and trials lying ahead of us as we move into the final phase of this present age. Therefore we need to follow the example of the leaders of the early church: to come and sit at the feet of Jesus to hear the word He has for us.

Having an ear to hear

The reason why we as believers have great problems in hearing the voice of God is not that we do not have spiritual ears to hear with. Remember what Jesus told Nicodemus:

*"The wind blows where it wishes, and you hear the sound of it, but cannot tell where it comes from and where it goes. **So is everyone who is born of the Spirit**."*

(John 3:8, emphasis added)

This clearly means that everyone who is born again is born with an ear to hear the sound, the voice, of the Holy Spirit. Is this not also what we learn from this word of the Lord Jesus?

"And when he brings out his own sheep, he goes before them; and the sheep follow him, for they know his voice."

(John 10:4)

He was speaking about the way a shepherd leads his sheep. And later He talks about how He, the Good Shepherd, leads His flock:

"My sheep hear My voice, and I know them, and they follow Me."   (John 10:27)

We can conclude from this that every true child of God has been equipped with the ability to hear the voice of God.

The problem is that we can have an ear to hear and still not hear the voice of God. One reason for this is simply that we don't give time to sit at His feet and listen. We have not moved to a place where we, like Mary, are giving the Lord our undivided attention. We are more like Martha running around being busy with a lot of things. We must learn to consecrate our ears to the Lord.

From the Old Testament we learn that when a servant was offered to be released from his commitment to his master (something that the law demanded any master to do after six years of service), and the servant nevertheless wanted to stay with his master, the servant had to undergo a certain ritual to be consecrated for service to his master forever:

"But if the servant plainly says, 'I love my master, my wife and my children; I will not go out free,' then his master shall bring him to the judges. He shall also bring him to the door, or to the doorpost, and his master shall pierce his ear with an awl, and he shall serve him forever."   (Exodus 21:5–6)

It is not enough to know that we have been born with the ability to hear. We need to consecrate our spiritual ears to the Lord knowing that our ears as well as our whole body

belong to Him. Paul beseeches us to consecrate our whole
being to the Lord:

> *"I beseech you therefore, brethren, by the mercies of God, that*
> *you present your bodies a living sacrifice, holy, acceptable to*
> *God, which is your reasonable service."*   (Romans 12:1)

This is what the Lord Jesus did when He entered into this
world:

> *"Therefore, when He came into the world, He said:*
>
> > *'Sacrifice and offering You did not desire,*
> > *But a body You have prepared for Me.*
> > *In burnt offerings and sacrifices for sin*
> > *You had no pleasure.*
> > *Then I said, "Behold, I have come –*
> > *In the volume of the book it is written of Me –*
> > *To do Your will, O God!"'"*   (Hebrews 10:5–7)

This is a quotation from Psalm 40:6–8. Here the wording is
slightly different, but the meaning exactly the same:

> *"Sacrifice and offering You did not desire;*
> *My ears you have opened.*
> *Burnt offering and sin offering You did not require.*
> *Then I said, 'Behold, I come;*
> *In the scroll of the book it is written of me,*
> *I delight to do your will, O my God,*
> *And Your law is within my heart.'"*

Again and again in the Old Testament God is calling out to
the people of Israel to "lend Him their ear".

If we are ever going to be able to hear from God we need to
commit ourselves to come and sit at Jesus' feet and take the
time needed to listen until we hear His word to us.

Being dull to hear

Another problem of hearing is described by the author of the letter to the Hebrews. Speaking about the Messiah he says:

> "... *of whom we have much to say, and hard to explain, since you have become dull of hearing.*"   (Hebrews 5:11)

The problem here is that God's people have heard so much without obeying God's voice and His Word. They have become so used to hearing without taking note of what the Lord was saying that in the end their ability to hear has been greatly reduced. This is why the letter to the Hebrews continues to say:

> "*For though by this time you ought to be teachers, you need someone to teach you again the first principles of the oracles of God; and you have come to need milk and not solid food.*"
> (Hebrews 5:12)

This is the severe judgment the Lord put on His people:

> "*Hearing you will hear and shall not understand,*
> *And seeing you will see and not perceive;*
> *For the hearts of this people have grown dull.*
> *Their ears are hard of hearing.*"   (Matthew 13:14–15)

How we need to ask the Lord to clean out our ears from all that has blocked them causing us to lose our sense of hearing the Holy Spirit; just as we also now and then need to clean out our physical ears from an overdose of wax. I remember from my childhood how my brother and I sometimes could not hear our mother calling us, simply because we did not have clean ears.

The prophet Isaiah speaks about how we need the Lord to open our ears:

"The Lord GOD has given Me
The tongue of the learned,
That I should know how to speak
A word in season to him who is weary.
He awakens Me morning by morning,
He awakens My ear
To hear as the learned.
The Lord GOD has opened My ear:
And I was not rebellious,
Nor did I turn away."   (Isaiah 50:4–5)

This is obviously a prophetic word referring to the Son of God, relating what He said in Psalm 40 about God having opened His ear.

The interesting thing is that the word being used here for opening the ear literally in Hebrew means "He has dug out my ear" – as with the use of a sharp instrument! And the context shows that for God to give us opened ears He sometimes has to use difficult circumstances. It is not an easy thing to be able to hear from God and as our ears so often are stuffed with all kinds of things that make us dull of hearing we need the Lord to perform an operation – and that can be rather painful.

Listen to this solemn word of the Lord:

"I will instruct you and teach you in the way you should go;
I will guide you with My eye.
Do not be like the horse or like the mule,
Which have no understanding,
Which must be harnessed with bit and bridle,
Else they will not come near you."   (Psalm 32:8–9)

May we humble ourselves before God in repentance and ask Him to open our ears to hear His word. May we drop all other things and rush to the feet of the Lord Jesus to listen to His word!

Entering His Rest

Chapter 8

Rest Is to Know the Lord

The substance of eternal life is to know the Lord. This is the way the Lord Jesus defines what eternal life is:

> *"And this is eternal life, that they may know You, the only true God, and Jesus Christ, whom You have sent."*
>
> (John 17:3)

Growing in the knowledge of who the Lord is will bring a deep sense of rest and stability to the life of the believer. In a time of increased unrest and trouble in the world we really need to come to a deeper knowledge of who the Lord is. We are moving more and more into what the Bible calls the anti-Christian period that comes shortly before the return of the Lord Jesus Christ.

The book of Daniel portrays the great pressures and difficulties for the believers such a time will bring to bear upon the earth. But it also tells us that in the midst of it all those believers who know their God shall overcome it all:

> *"And forces shall be mustered by him* [the antichrist], *and they shall defile the sanctuary fortress; then they shall take away the daily sacrifices, and place there the abomination of desolation* [see Matthew 24:15–28]. *Those who do wickedly against the covenant he shall corrupt with flattery; but the*

*people who know their God shall be strong, and carry out great
exploits."*   (Daniel 11:31–32)

Knowing God will be the only way to be victorious through
the tough circumstances the people of God will encounter in
these last days. That is the key to be able to enjoy true rest
in the midst of whatever is going on in the world.

To know God as the rock

The disciple Peter was the most impulsive, superficial and
unstable person until he came to know who the Lord really
was. He had a big mouth and talked again and again about
how he would always be faithful to his Lord and never forsake
Him even when the Lord announced that He would have to
go to the cross and die. Of course when it finally came to it
Peter betrayed Jesus and went through a very deep crisis in
his life:

> *"And the Lord said, 'Simon, Simon! Indeed, Satan has asked
> for you, that he may sift you as wheat. But I have prayed for
> you, that your faith should not fail; and when you have
> returned to Me, strengthen your brethren.'*
>
> *But he [Peter] said to Him: 'Lord, I am ready to go with You,
> both to prison and to death.'*
>
> *Then He said: 'I tell you, Peter, the rooster shall not crow
> this day before you will deny three times that you know Me.'"*
> (Luke 22:31–34)

Jesus had already taught Simon Peter that as he came to know
who He was he would be changed from his unstable and
impulsive nature into a stable and firm person becoming
partaker of divine nature:

> *"He said to them, 'But who do you say that I am?'*
>
> *Simon Peter answered and said: 'You are the Christ, the Son
> of the living God.'*

> *Jesus answered and said to him: 'Blessed are you, Simon Bar-Jonah, for flesh and blood has not revealed this to you, but My Father who is in heaven. And I also say to you that you are Peter, and on this rock I will build My church, and the gates of Hades shall not prevail against it.'"*
>
> (Matthew 16:15–18)

This is a remarkable word by the Lord Jesus, a word we need to try to understand. After Simon Peter's confession Jesus gives him a new identity. He is now to be "Peter" which in Greek is *Petros*, a piece of the rock. Peter is not the rock (Greek: *petra*) upon which Jesus will build His church. We know that Jesus Himself is the rock upon which the church is built. There is no other foundation. This is overwhelmingly clear in all Scripture. God would never dare to build His church on any human being. What Jesus therefore says here is that through the revelation which He is given by His heavenly Father to Peter, he, Peter, has become a part of Christ, the rock. He has become a partaker of divine nature through faith in the living Son of God.

Later in Peter's experience we see how he has come to know in depth who the Lord really is. Remember the story from the book of Acts, chapter 12. After King Herod had killed James, he saw that it pleased the crowd, so he arrested Peter and put him in prison. Of course his intention was to also kill Peter. Here we join the story:

> *"Peter was therefore kept in prison, but constant prayer was offered to God for him by the church. And when Herod was about to bring him out, that night Peter was sleeping, bound with two chains between two soldiers; and the guards before the door were keeping the prison. Now behold, an angel of the Lord stood by him, and a light shone in the prison; and he struck Peter on the side and raised him up, saying: 'Arise quickly!' And his chains fell off his hands."*
>
> (Acts 12:5–7)

What I want to point out here is not so much the wonder of this miraculous deliverance of Peter from the prison. It is this astonishing thing that Peter was able to sleep soundly in the prison knowing that he most surely would have been killed the next day just like James was, had it not been for the Lord's intervention. How would any of us have felt if we knew that this was our last night and tomorrow we would be executed? Peter certainly had come to know the Lord so deeply that he was able to sleep "like a rock" under such circumstances. He enjoyed full peace and rest knowing that the Lord was in full control.

Knowing the Lord as the *rock* is a key to inner peace and rest. Even David knew the Lord this way and could sing:

> *"Truly my soul silently waits for God;*
> *From Him comes my salvation.*
> *He only is my rock and my salvation;*
> *He is my defense;*
> *I shall not be greatly moved."*   (Psalm 62:1–2)

Knowing God as love

The enemy will always try to steal our peace by claiming that God does not love us, because: Just look what we have to go through! He is trying to fill us with fear and anxiety.

In the story in John's gospel chapter 11 about the sickness of Lazarus, the brother of Mary and Martha, it is clearly stated that *"Jesus loved Martha and her sister and Lazarus"* (verse 5).

It was not easy for the sisters to see though, because Jesus knowing that Lazarus was sick did not go to visit for another couple of days. And when he finally came Lazarus had died and was already buried. As Jesus met with Martha, she complained that if Jesus had come earlier Lazarus would not have died. When Jesus replied that Lazarus would rise again, Martha pointed to the resurrection at the last day, meaning at the end of the age. Jesus then said: *"I am the resurrection and the* life" (verse 25), underlining the fact that resurrection is present in Him here and now. Martha did not know the Lord that well. If she had she would not have regretted Jesus' late arrival and would not have been anxious and sad over her brother's death. Knowing God as love brings an assurance and a deep rest into our souls. God cannot do other than love us whatever our circumstances may be.

The reason for our fears is the fact that we do not know that God is love. This is the testimony of the apostle John:

> *"There is no fear in love; but perfect love casts out fear, because fear involves torment. But he who fears has not been made perfect in love."* (1 John 4:18)

Abraham is the perfect example of one who knew God in a deep and trusting way. When God ordered him to bring his son Isaac, the one God had given him in the first place as his heir, he obeyed the Lord and took his son with him up upon Mount Moriah and tied him to the altar, ready to kill him. This was the utmost test that anyone could ever be exposed to. How could God give him the son of promise and then ask him to sacrifice him? And how could Abraham be ready to bring his son as a sacrifice knowing that Isaac was God's elected heir to him? The scripture is clear. Abraham knew God so well that he was fully convinced that if he had to kill Isaac God would have to raise him again from the dead:

> *"By faith Abraham, when he was tested, offered up Isaac, and he who had received the promises offered up his only begotten son, of whom it was said, 'In Isaac your seed shall be called,' concluding that God was able to raise him up, even from the dead, from which he also received him in a figurative sense."*
> (Hebrews 11:17–19)

Knowing God is love will always give us an inner peace and rest even in situations that are completely impossible.

Knowing God is faithful

God's character is firm and unchangeable. He cannot be any other than the One He is. Paul explains it this way:

> *"This is a faithful saying . . .*
>
> *If we are faithless,*
> *He remains faithful;*
> *He cannot deny Himself."*   (2 Timothy 2:11, 13)

Nothing can give us a deeper sense of peace, trust and rest than knowing that God is always faithful to His Word and His promises. He is fully unable to change His nature and character.

The well known English missionary Hudson Taylor had a personal experience of that while he was in China. He always used to say that his mission work was a faith mission. At a certain time in his work he entered into a time of depression. He seemed to have lost faith in his mission and wrote back to the leadership of China Inland Mission in London that he had become a failure and should never had gone to China. The mission in England sent emergency prayer requests to all their supporters. One day when Hudson Taylor was sitting in his house and having a cup of tea, he had his Bible lying on a side table. He had not been reading the Word of God for a long time. But almost by accident he reached out for his Bible and when he opened it his eyes caught this word from 2 Timothy 2:13: *"If we are faithless, He remains faithful; He cannot deny Himself!"* The words hit him like a hammer, and he began to understand what a great mistake he had made in stressing that his mission was one of faith. If our work is based on our faith or any human being's faith it is bound to fail sooner or later. Hudson Taylor turned to God and confessed his sin. He was fully restored and ever after he always proclaimed that his mission was based solely on God's faithfulness. After this the China Inland Mission's work in China grew tremendously.

Knowing God as faithful is a key to be able to stand and to work with confidence and peace through all circumstances.

This is what the Lord said about His people of Israel:

> " 'For I am the LORD, I do not change;
> Therefore you are not consumed, O sons of Jacob.
> Yet from the days of your fathers
> You have gone away from My ordinances
> And have not kept them.
> Return to Me and I will return to you,'
> Says the LORD of Hosts."   (Malachi 3:6–7)

The whole future of the people of Israel is not dependent on their works or efforts. It rests entirely on God's faithfulness. And in the end the Lord will fulfill every word and every promise He made to Abraham and his descendants. As the battle continues and gets even fiercer and worse this is the only place of rest and trust we have. God is faithful. He cannot change, because He cannot deny Himself.

Chapter 9

Rest Is to See as God Sees

The letter to the Hebrews speaks about the need for the believers to enter into the rest of the Lord (Hebrews 4:1–9). This rest is compared to the Sabbath rest when the writer refers to the fact that God rested on the seventh day after having finished His work of creating heaven and earth:

> *"For He has spoken in a certain place of the seventh day in this way: 'And God rested on the seventh day from all His works.'"*
> (Hebrews 4:4)

The text speaks about the generation of Israelites in the wilderness who because of disobedience were not allowed to enter the promised land. According to these verses from Hebrews that meant that they did not enter the rest of the Lord. We, the New Testament believers, are now challenged to enter into the Shabbat rest of God:

> *"There remains therefore a rest for the people of God. For he who has entered His rest has himself also ceased from his works as God did from His."*   (Hebrews 4:9–10)

It is clear that we are to enter into God's rest. That means that we are to rest the same way God is resting. In order to know how to do that we need to know how God is resting. God worked for six days and rested on the seventh. How does He maintain His rest?

The answer we find on the first pages of the Bible:

> *"Then God saw everything that He had made, and indeed it was very good."*   (Genesis 1:31)

> *"And on the seventh day God ended His work which He had done, and He rested on the seventh day from all His work which He had done. The God blessed the seventh day and sanctified it, because in it He rested from all His work, which God had created and made."*   (Genesis 2:2–3)

God finished His work and He looked at it and saw that it was very good. It was perfect! God is resting in all that He made, and the way He enjoys and maintains His rest is by constantly looking at it. If we are to rest like God, we too have to learn to look at the finished work of God.

Looking at that which God looks at

How does God look at the troubled world situation? How does the Lord react to all the rebellion, all the violence and all the sinfulness of this ungodly generation?

Psalm 2 brings the answer:

> *"Why do the nations rage,*
> *And the people plot a vain thing?*
> *The kings of the earth set themselves,*
> *And the rulers take counsel together,*
> *Against the* Lord *and against His Anointed, saying,*
> *'Let us break Their bonds in pieces*
> *And cast away Their cords from us.'*
> *He who sits in the heavens shall laugh;*
> *The* Lord *shall hold them in derision.*
> *Then He shall speak to them in His wrath,*
> *And distress them in His deep displeasure:*

'Yet I have set My King
On My holy hill of Zion.
I will declare the decree:
The LORD *has said to Me,*
"You are My Son,
Today I have begotten You.
Ask of Me, and I will give You
The nations for Your inheritance,
And the ends of the earth for Your possession." ' "

(Psalm 2:1–8)

It appears to me that God is not at all anxious or troubled about what the leaders of the world are up to. There is a worldwide rebellion underway where the leaders of the nations are trying to get rid of God and of His Word. They will not accept God's authority or His ownership to this world which He created. The Lord laughs! He simply cannot understand why the kings and princes of this world are making all this noise. The Lord sits on His throne and laughs. He is fully relaxed and has everything under control. He is enjoying perfect rest. Why? Because He has already settled the whole issue of who is the true Ruler of this earth and all the nations. Long ago He designated His Son to be the King of the earth and all the nations: *"I have set My King on My holy hill of Zion!"*

Who is this King? It is His Son, the Messiah, the Lord Jesus Christ!

The Father declares that to His Son, whom He has begotten, He has given *"the nations for Your inheritance, and the ends of the earth for Your possession"*.

The world rulers can do whatever they like. God has already settled the issue of world dominion. The Lord considers the finished work of His Son and He is resting in that. He is looking at His Son and the ultimate victory He has won once and for all.

If we want to enjoy resting in God we need to look at the same things God is looking at. We must constantly consider and look at the finished work of the Son of God.

How was Abraham, our father in the faith, able to keep his peace as he lived as a foreigner in the land God had given him? In his lifetime he never came to own any of the land, but had to move around like a pilgrim, living in tents. The secret to his inward rest was that he looked at that which God had prepared:

> *"for he waited for the city which has foundations, whose builder and maker is God."*   (Hebrews 11:10)

Abraham kept before his eyes the finished work of God: the eternal city of the New Jerusalem.

God's finished work in Christ

God is resting, because His works were finished from the foundation of the world (Hebrews 4:3).

It is an amazing biblical truth that the finished work of God in Christ was accomplished before the foundation of the world. It is not easy for us to understand because we are limited by time and history. God is eternal and above all limitations of time and matter.

We being chosen for salvation is no recent thing. It actually happened before the foundation of the world according to Ephesians 1:4:

> *" ... He chose us in Him before the foundation of the world, that we should be holy and without blame before Him in love."*

Not only was our election decided a long time ago. Even our very life here on earth is not by accident. It was prepared and planned a long time ago:

> *"For we are His workmanship, created in Christ Jesus for good works, which God prepared beforehand that we should walk in them."*   (Ephesians 2:10)

The word "beforehand" here is in the original the word "before time".

What I want to say with these statements is that when the Word of God says that God has finished His work it is not only true about the physical creation. It is also about God's spiritual work of providing salvation for all those who believe. It is what the Lord Jesus confirmed when on the cross He proclaimed: *"It is finished!"* (John 19:30, emphasis added).

When we turn our eyes away from the physical things of this world and look upon the finished work of God, we can enjoy the same rest as the Lord is enjoying.

Chapter 10

Rest Is to Surrender All

Jesus gave His disciples an important teaching about how they could live and walk in the rest of God:

> *"At that time Jesus answered and said: 'I thank You, Father, Lord of heaven and earth, that you have hidden these things from the wise and prudent and have revealed them to babes. Even so, Father, for so it seemed good in Your sight. All things have been delivered to Me by My Father, and no one know the Son except the Father. Nor does anyone know the Father except the Son, and the one to whom the Son wills to reveal Him. Come to Me, all you who labor and are heavy laden, and I will give you rest. Take My yoke upon you and learn from Me, for I am gentle and lowly in heart, and you will find rest for your souls. For My yoke is easy and My burden is light.'"*
>
> (Matthew 11:25–30)

The Lord is showing us here how we might have rest and find rest in our entire walk in life. This is something of a secret that Jesus is bringing to us. It requires that we receive a certain revelation, a revelation that is hidden from the wise and prudent, but open to those who have the attitude of a child. We often think that the way to real inner peace and rest comes through having as much head knowledge about spiritual things as possible. The more we get answers to our many questions the more we shall come to rest in our mind. The truth is that trying to understand everything and get answers to all our problems in fact creates more burdens and unrest in our souls. Those who want to be so very wise often become full of anxieties and end up as the most tense and insecure people of all.

There is a most unusual word for this in the book of Ecclesiastes 1:18:

> *"For in much wisdom is much grief,*
> *And he who increases knowledge increases*
>   *sorrow."*

We do not find rest for our souls by constantly exercising our brain wanting to understand everything and wrestling to get an answer to every question. There is a better way laid out for us in the book of Proverbs:

> *"Trust in the LORD with all your heart,*
> *And lean not on your own understanding;*
> *In all your ways acknowledge Him,*
> *And He shall direct your paths."*   (Proverbs 3:5–6)

As Jesus points out to us: we need to be like babes, to have that childlike attitude of trust and openness, if we want to receive spiritual revelation. We need to be like David, the King, who wrote in Psalm 131:

> *"LORD, my heart is not haughty,*
> *Nor my eyes lofty.*
> *Neither do I concern myself with great matters,*
> *Nor with things too profound for me.*
> *Surely I have calmed and quieted my soul,*
> *Like a weaned child with his mother;*

Like a weaned child is my soul within me.
O Israel, hope in the L*ORD*
From this time forth and forever."

Our ambitions to go after "great matters" trying to understand things that are too profound for us to grasp, make us
behave like an unweaned child. A child that has not yet been
weaned is full of tension and anxiety and is crying out for his
mother. He is full of fear that he will not get fed at the proper
time. Once the child has been weaned he relaxes, having
come to trust his mother that she will give him what he needs
at the proper time. The child has come to rest and knows that
he can fully trust the mother. This is the kind of "child" of
God we all need to be.

The revelation that brings rest

What is the revelation that Jesus speaks about?

It is that all things have been handed over to Him by His
Father. God has put His Son in charge of everything. He holds
the whole world, yes, and the whole universe in His hands. All
God's purposes and plans, all blessings, all power in heaven
and on earth, has been given over to the Son. Jesus confirms
that when He said to His disciples before He ascended into
heaven:

"All authority has been given to Me in heaven and on earth."
(Matthew 28:18)

It leaves nothing in our hands to do. Everything concerning
our life and faith now depends on a personal relationship with
the Son of God.

Since all things, on the part of God, have been handed over
to His Son, then our ability to have inner peace and rest is
dependent on whether we, likewise, are handing our all over
to His Son.

Rest is found in the yoke

The practical application of having this revelation is to follow the Lord's invitation to come to Him and take upon ourselves His yoke.

The Lord actually speaks about two kinds of rest here. He speaks about a rest He will give to us, if we come to Him. That rest is a gift of grace that we received when we came to the Lord and were saved. It is a rest of our spirit, a rest because we have been forgiven of all our sins and have been born again. This is a rest of salvation which we could never do anything to achieve. There is another rest, however, a rest for our souls. This rest depends on our willingness to follow the Lord and to take His yoke on ourselves.

For some time I thought that the yoke was a one-man yoke; the kind of yoke a person used in the old days to be able to carry heavy water buckets from the well. I therefore had a very negative feeling about taking up my cross and following Jesus. The yoke, however, is not a one-man thing. It is a two-man yoke. We are called to walk in the yoke with Christ. The picture here is that of two oxen yoked together to plough the field. Usually one grown-up, strong and experienced ox was put together with a young, wild and self-willed ox. The idea was to teach the younger one how to yield and submit to the leadership of the older one. It often took some time and a lot of trouble before the younger one would learn that it did not pay to react to the yoke, and to try to go its own way. The work would be much easier when he submitted and yielded to the yoke, so that together the pair could plough the field with the least possible effort.

When we come to Jesus and submit ourselves to Him, laying down our own will and way and following Him, He promises us that we will find rest for our souls. His yoke is easy and His burden is light. What we talk about here can also be expressed in the way Paul, the apostle, writes:

> *"I have been crucified with Christ; it is no longer I who live, but Christ lives in me; and the life which I now live in the flesh I*

live by faith in the Son of God, who loved me and gave Himself for me."   (Galatians 2:20)

Surrendering all of ourselves to the Lord and simply following Him will bring true rest for our souls.

Coming to sit at the feet of Jesus is a way to experience how to cease from our own works and enter into His rest.

Chapter 11

Blessings of Sitting at Jesus' Feet

Let us in closing consider some of the wonderful promises the Word of God offers to those who would come to sit at the feet of Jesus, meditate on His Word and wait on the Lord.

Power and strength

> *"Wait on the LORD;*
> *Be of good courage,*
> *And He shall strengthen your heart;*
> *Wait, I say, on the LORD!"* (Psalm 27:14)

Overflowing joy

> *"Our soul waits for the LORD;*
> *He is our help and our shield.*
> *For our heart shall rejoice in Him,*
> *Because we have trusted in His holy name."*
> (Psalm 33:20–21)

Deliverance

> *"I waited patiently for the LORD;*
> *And He inclined to me,*
> *And heard my cry.*

He also brought me up out of a horrible pit,
Out of the miry clay,
And set my feet upon a rock,
And established my steps.
He has put a new song in my mouth –
Praise to our God;
Many will see it and fear,
And will trust in the Lord*.''*   (Psalm 40:1–3)

Prosperity

''But I am like a green olive tree in the house of God;
I trust in the mercy of God forever and ever,
I will praise You forever,
Because You have done it;
And in the presence of Your saints
I will wait on Your name, for it is good.''   (Psalm 52:8–9)

Security

''Truly my soul silently waits for God;
From Him comes my salvation.
He is my rock and my salvation;
He is my defense;
I shall not be greatly moved.''

(Psalm 62:1–2)

Mercy

''My soul waits for the Lord
More than those who watch for the morning –
Yes, more than those who watch for the morning.
O Israel, hope in the Lord*;*
For with the Lord *there is mercy,*
And with Him is abundant redemption.
And He shall redeem Israel
From all his iniquities.''   (Psalm 130:6–8)